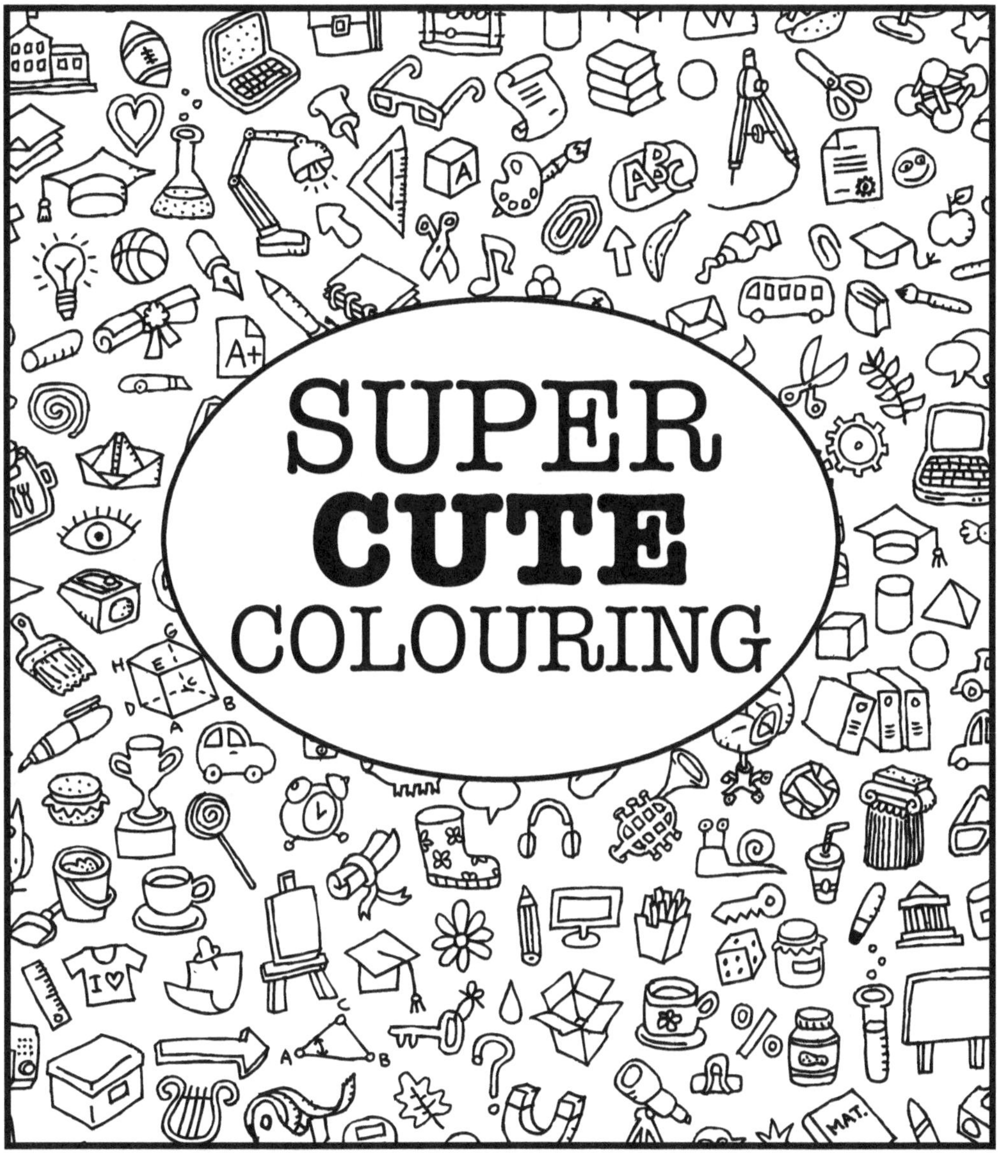

SUPER **CUTE** COLOURING

Gorgeous Colouring For Girls **Book 5**

First published in 2016 by Kyle Craig Publishing

Design: Elizabeth James, Julie Anson, Alison McNicol, Shutterstock, Inc.

ISBN: 978-1-78595-122-0

A CIP record for this book is available from the British Library.

A Kyle Craig Publication

www.kyle-craig.com

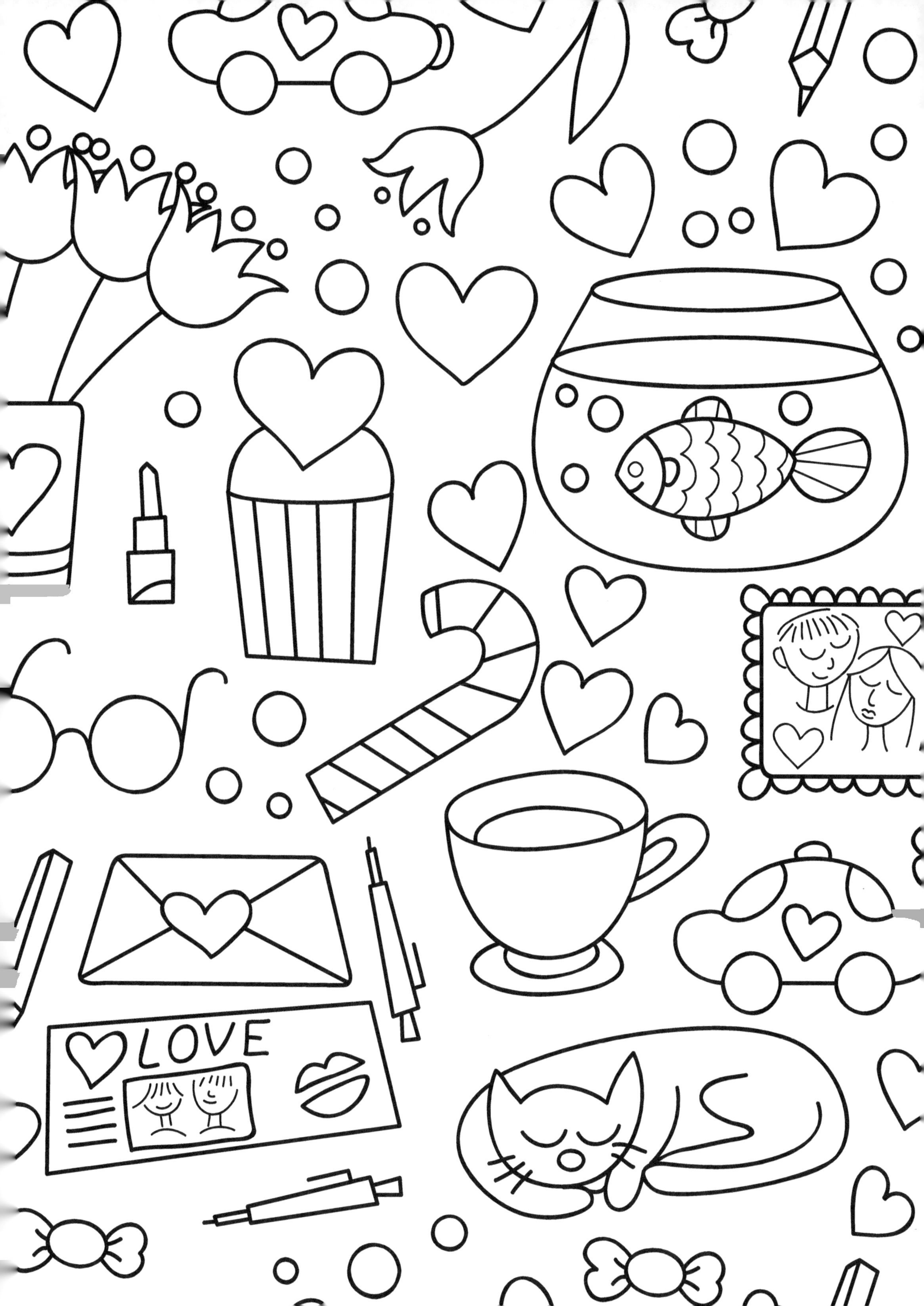
LOVE

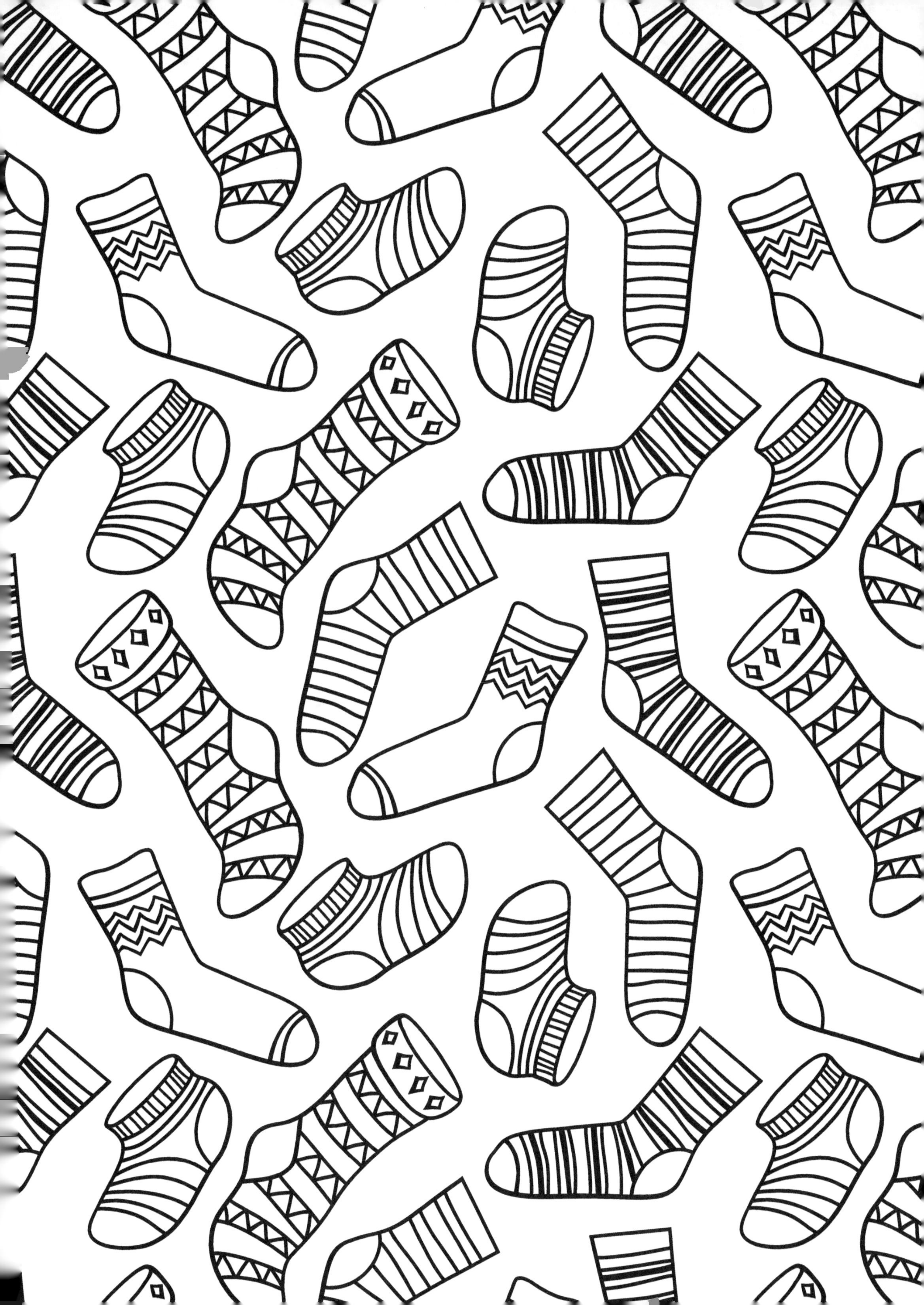

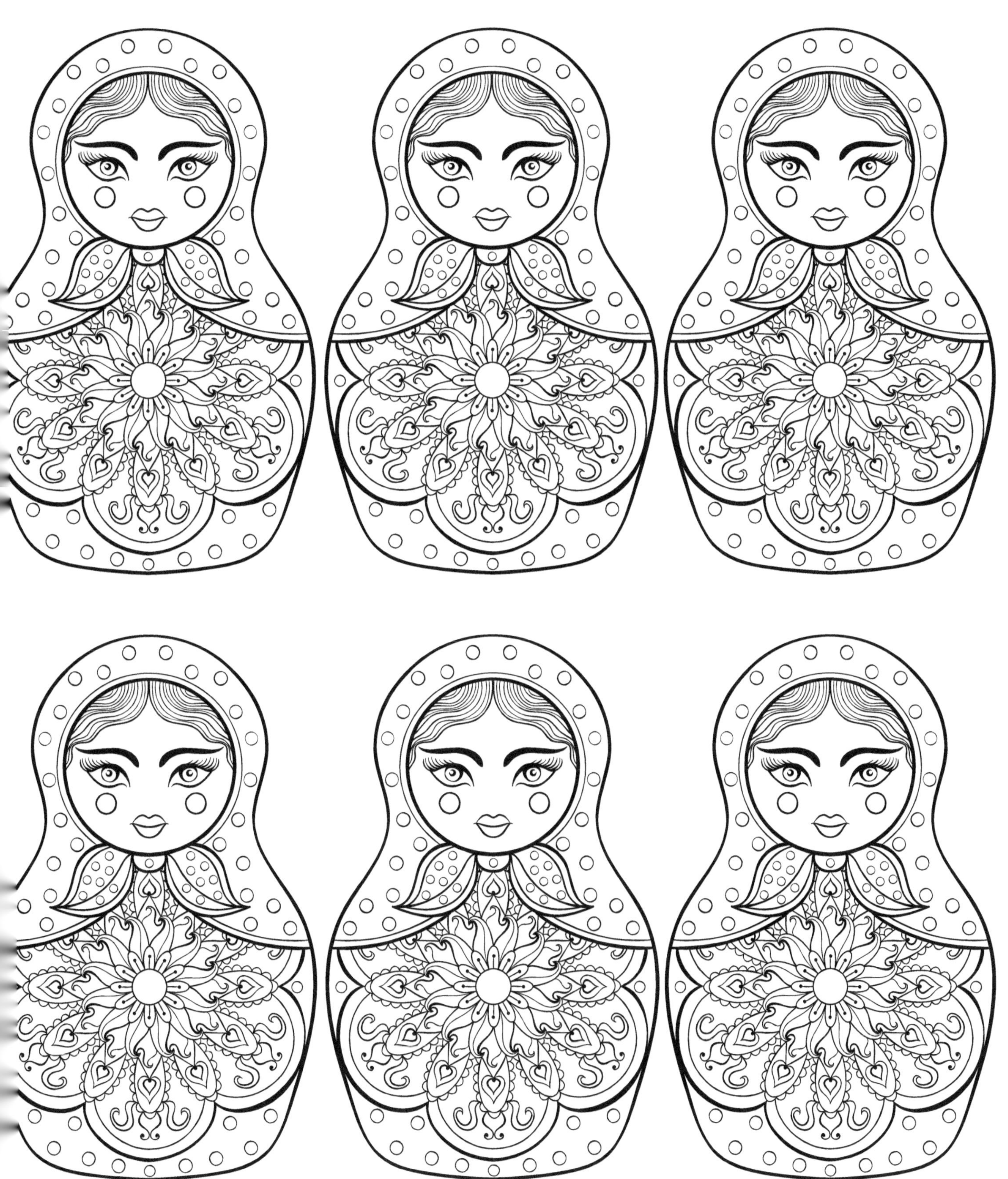

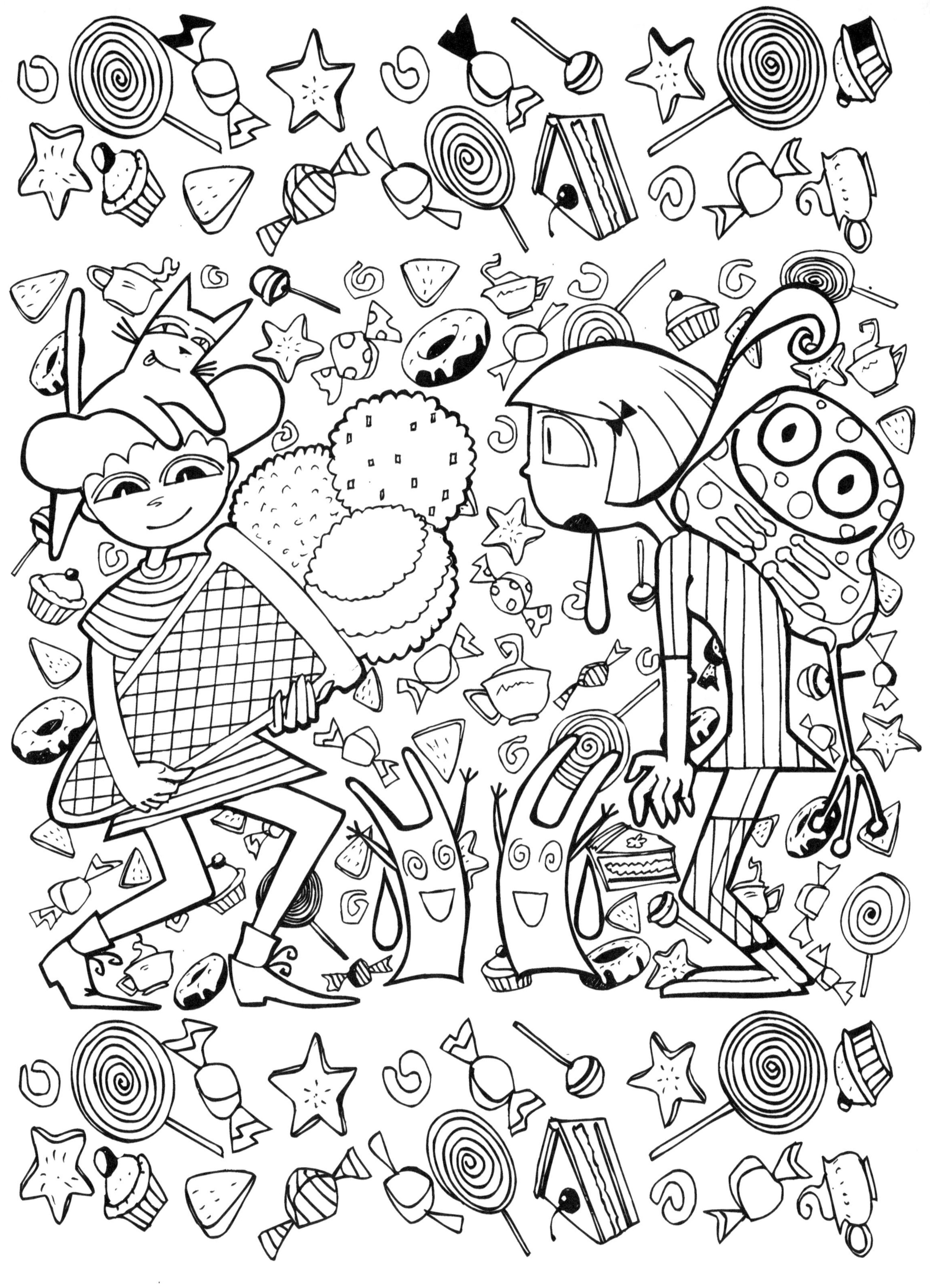

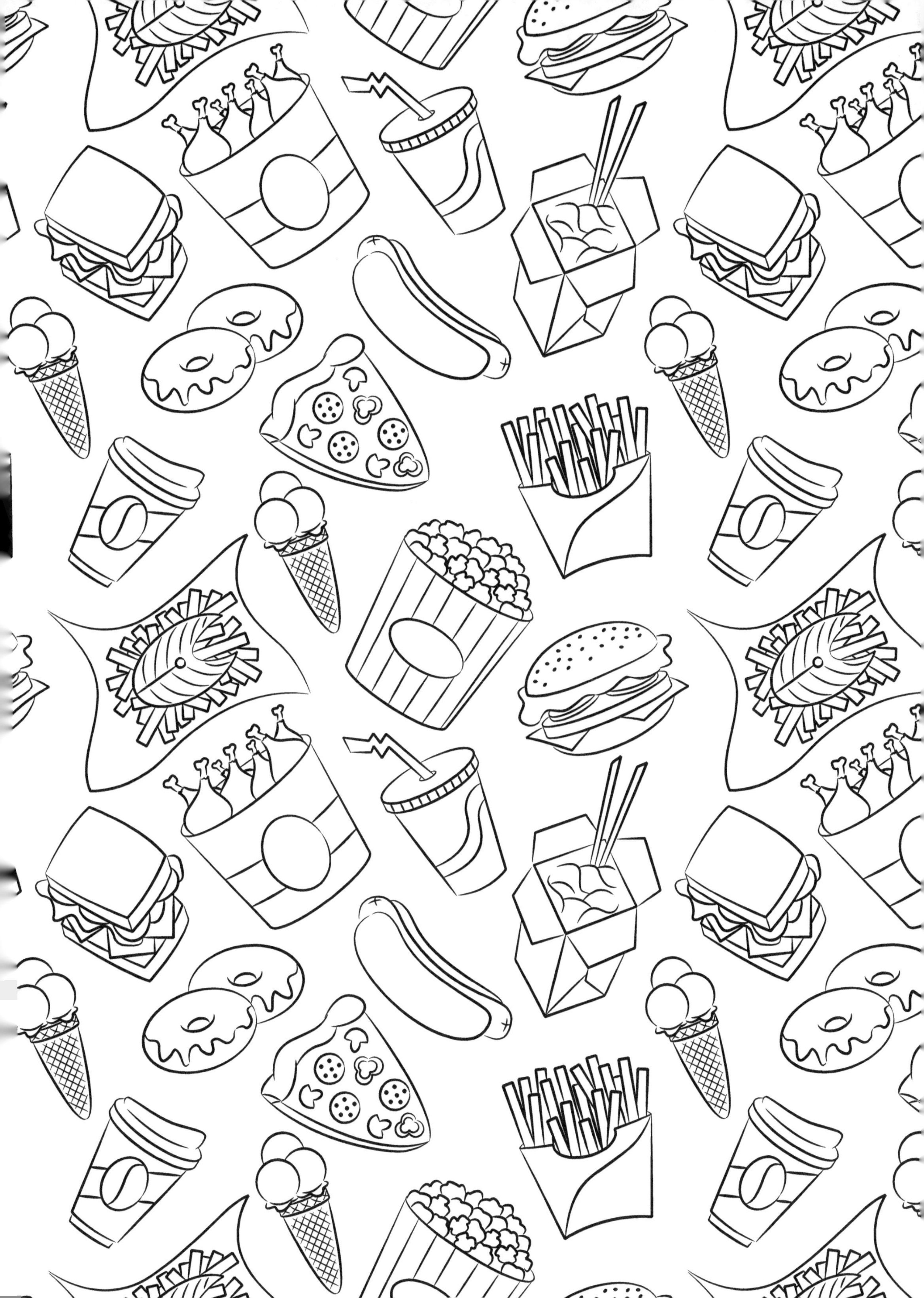

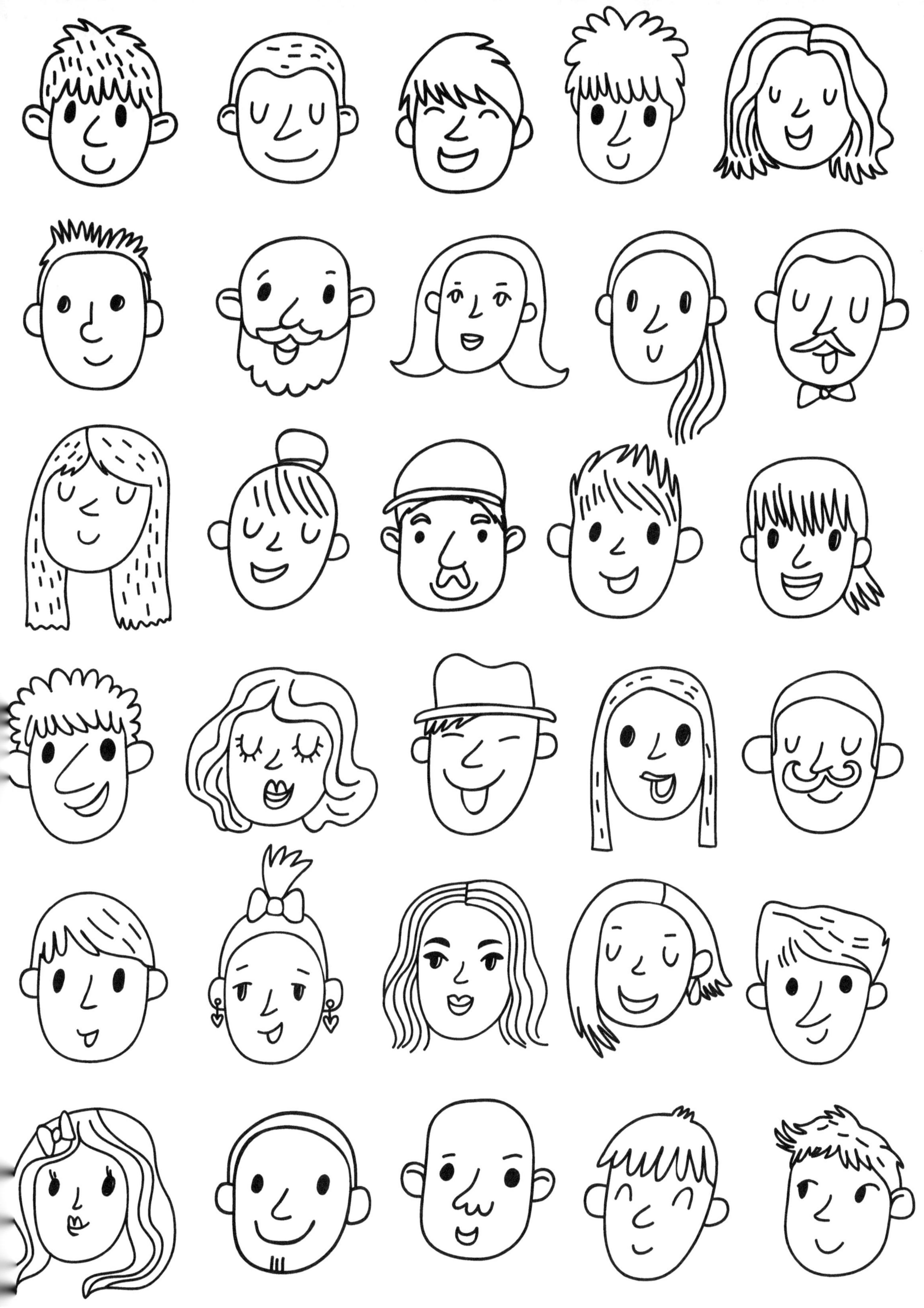

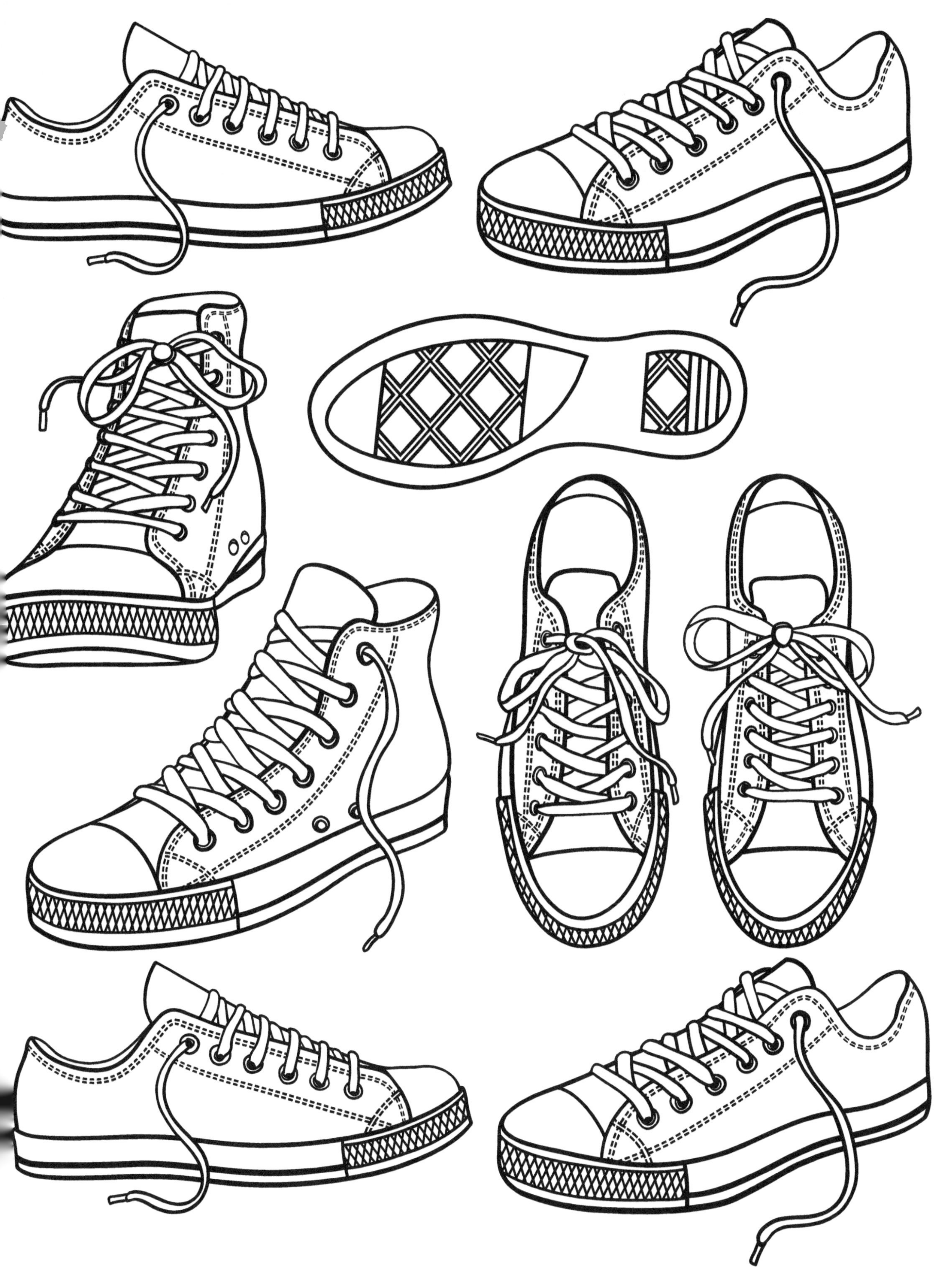

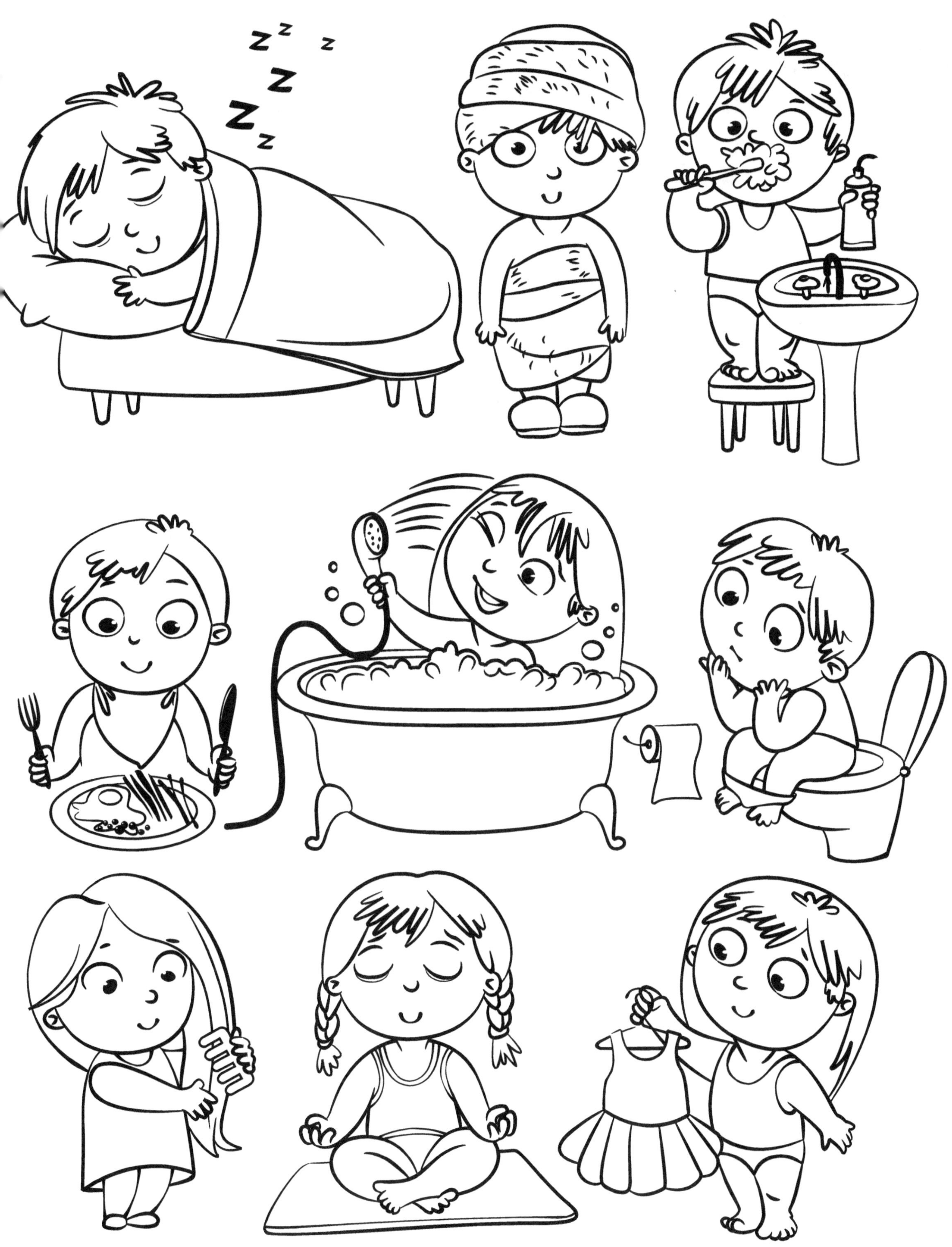
Z z z
Z
Z z

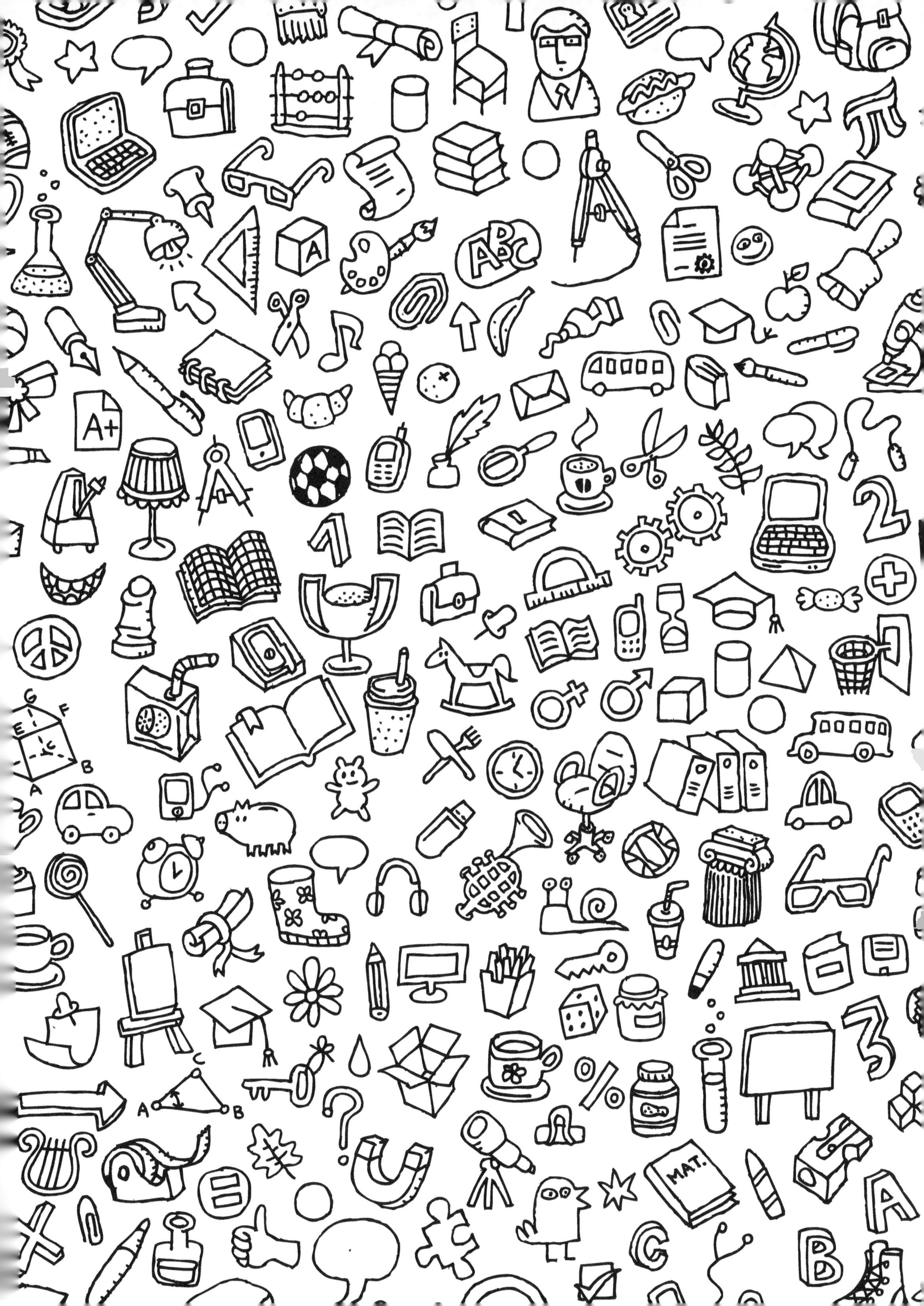
A+
MAT.

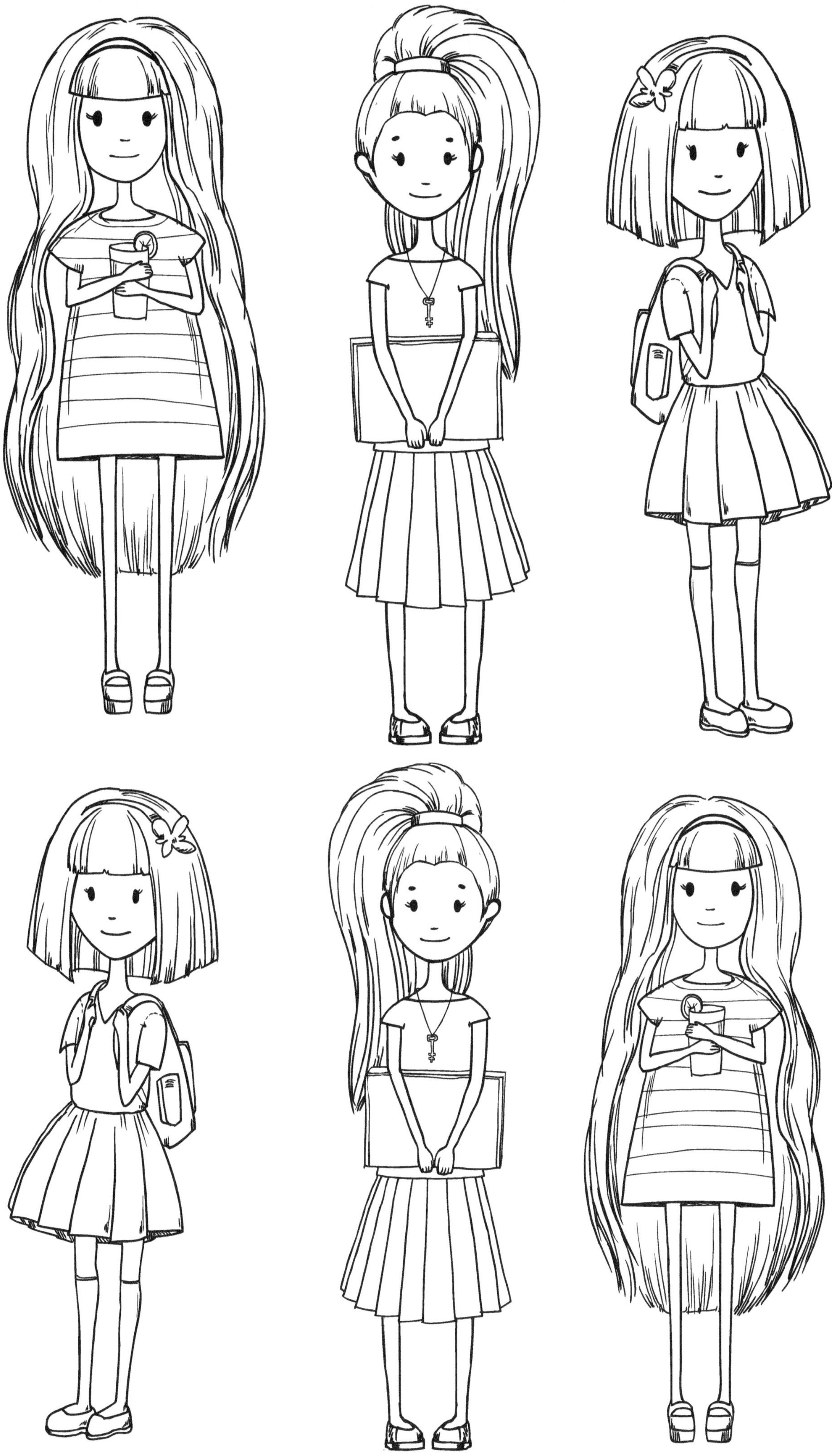

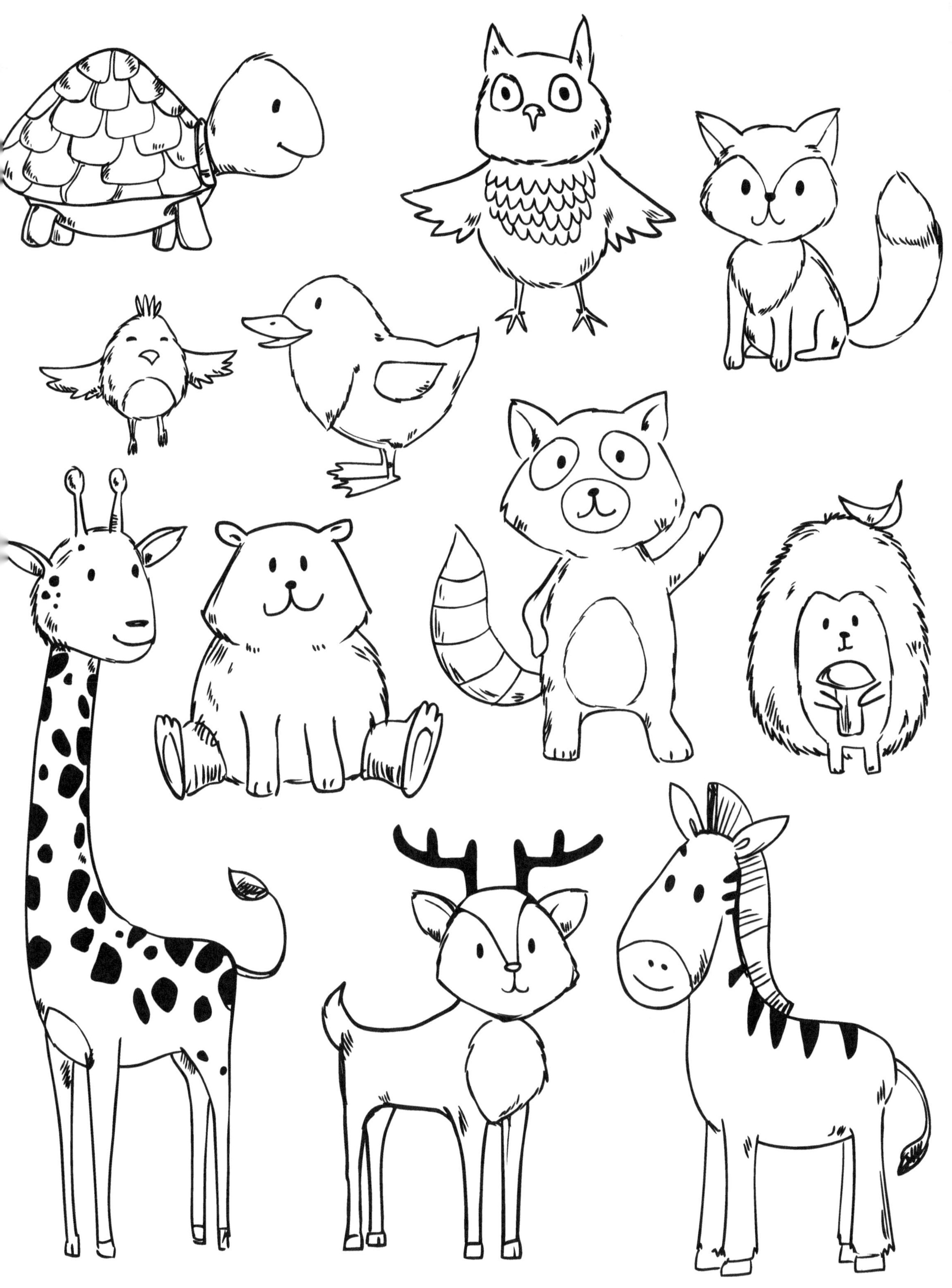

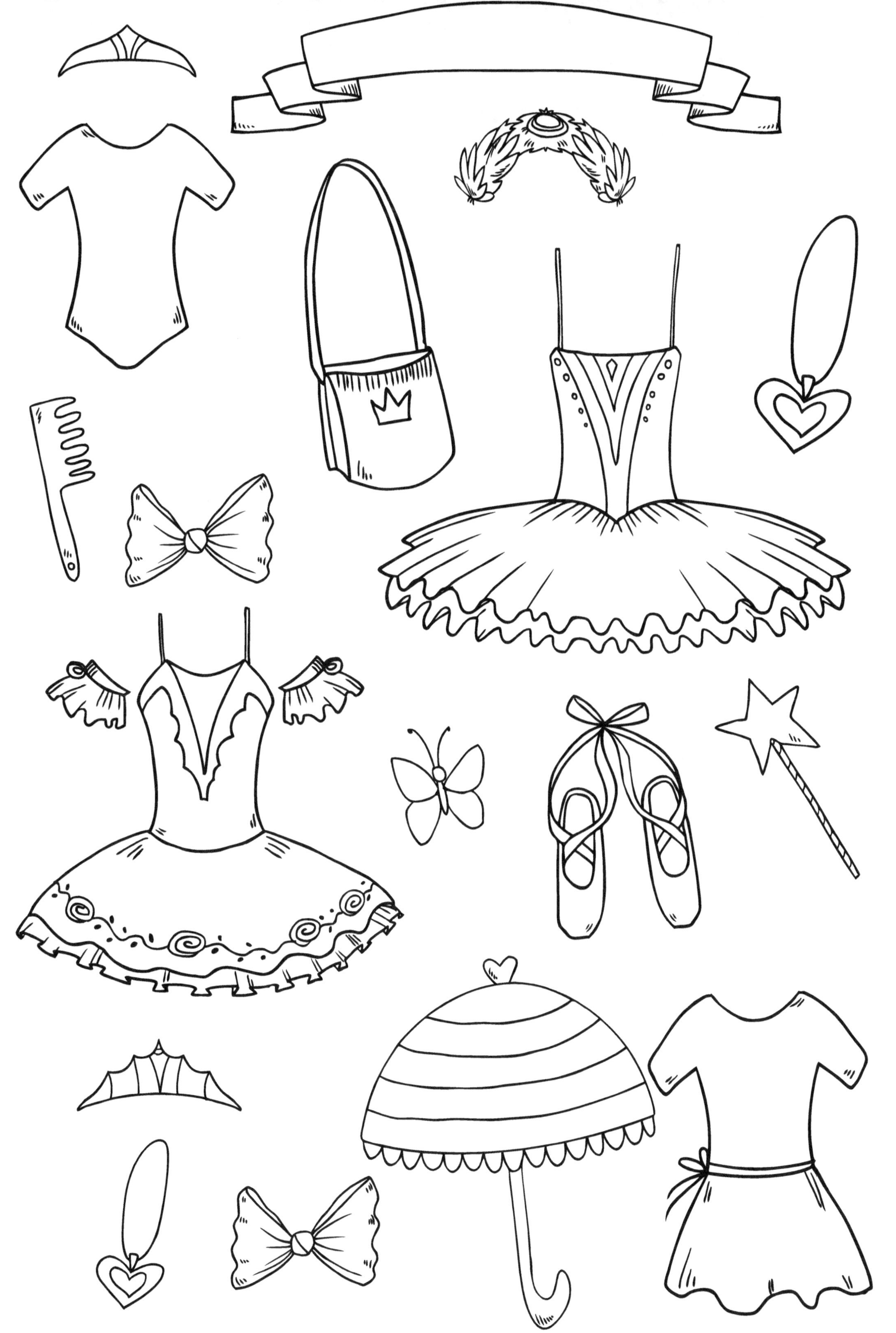

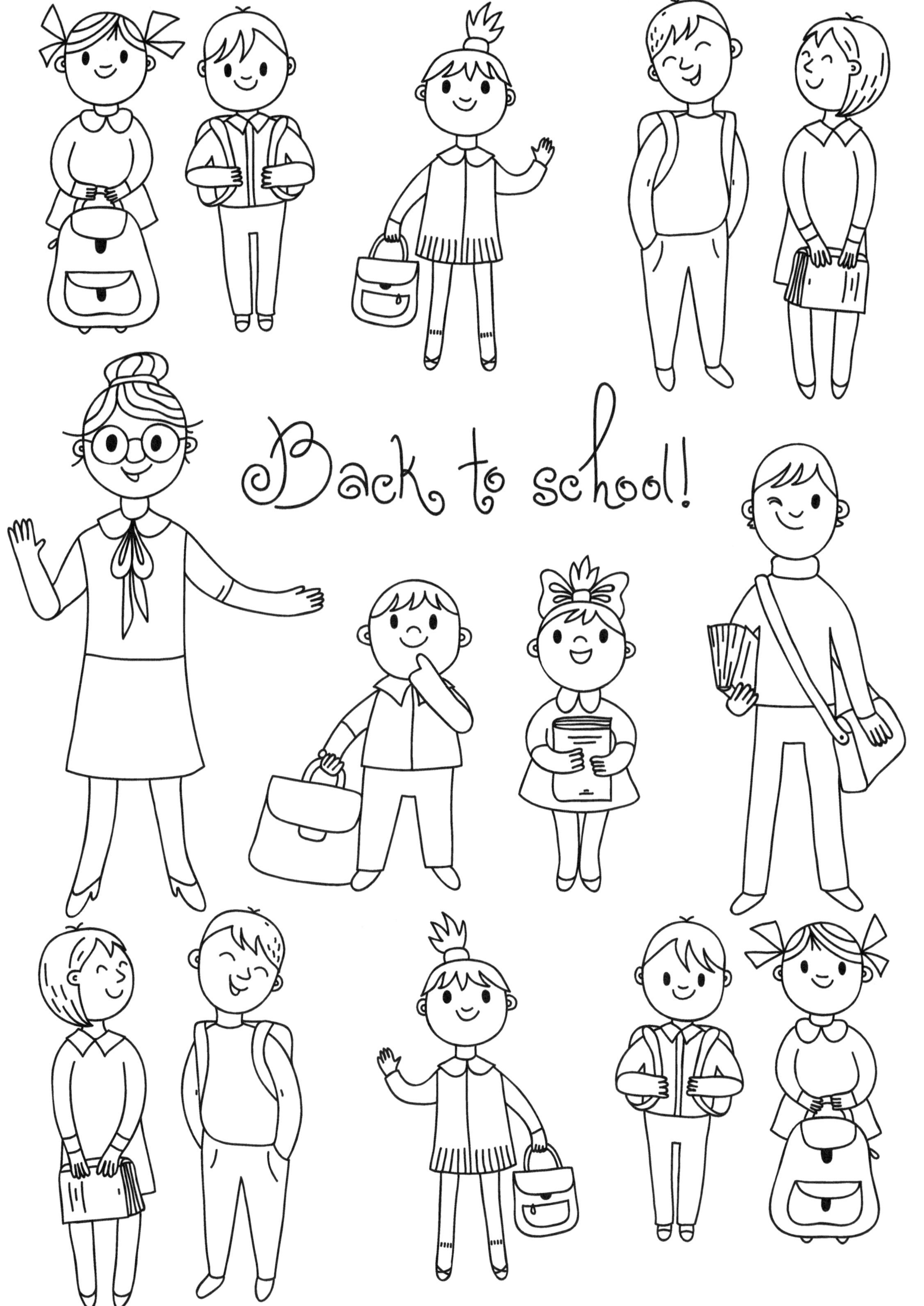
Back to school!

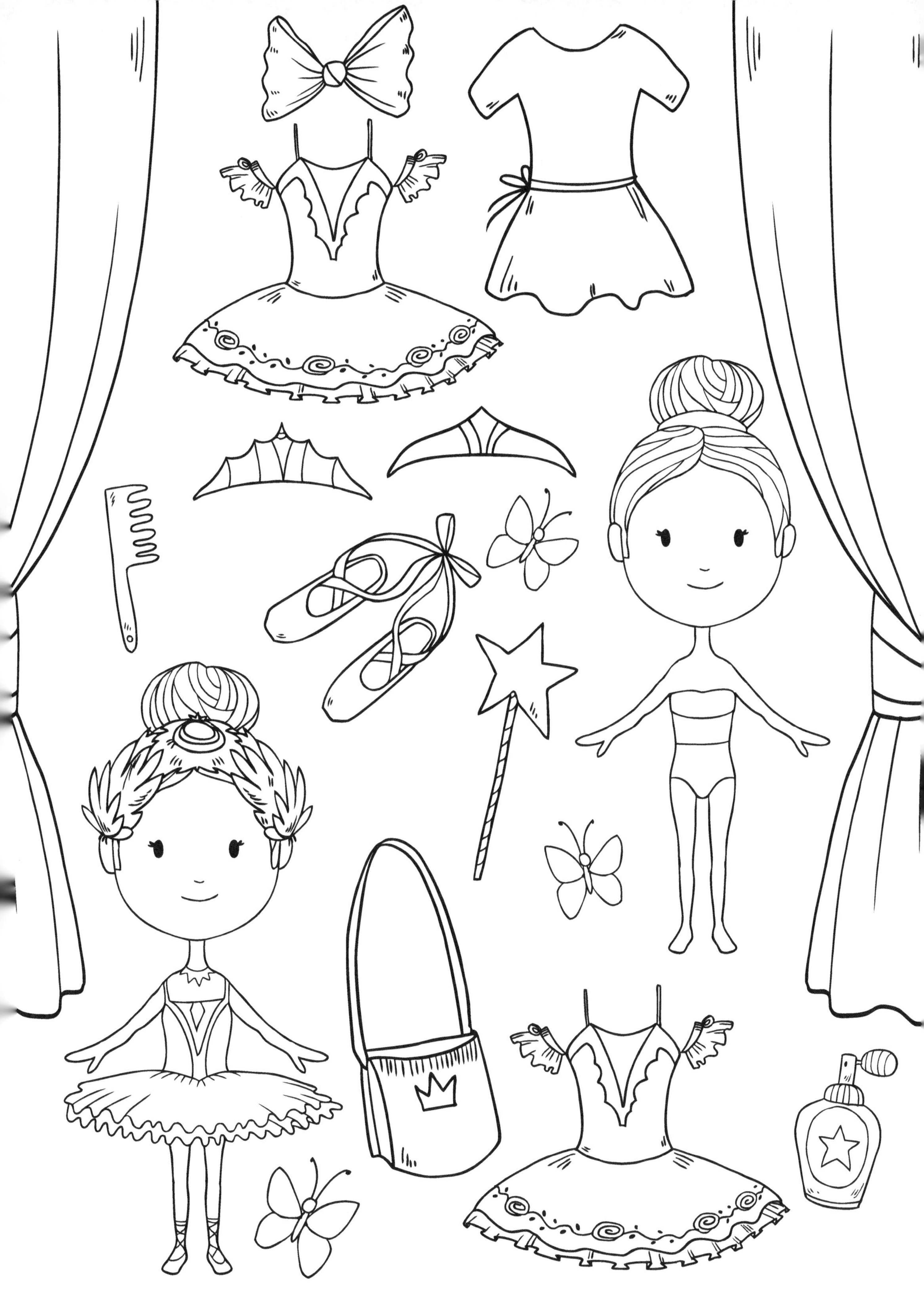

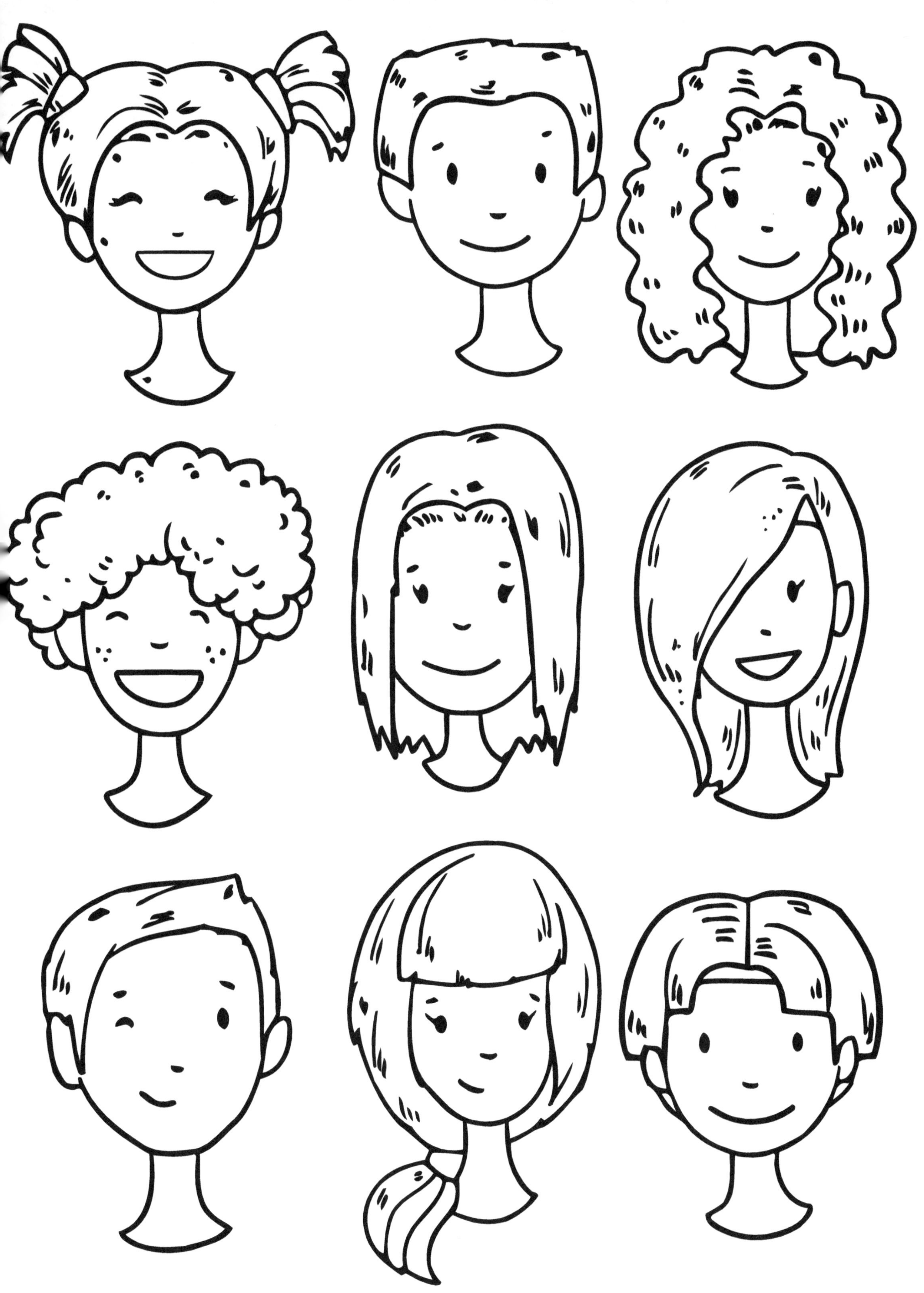

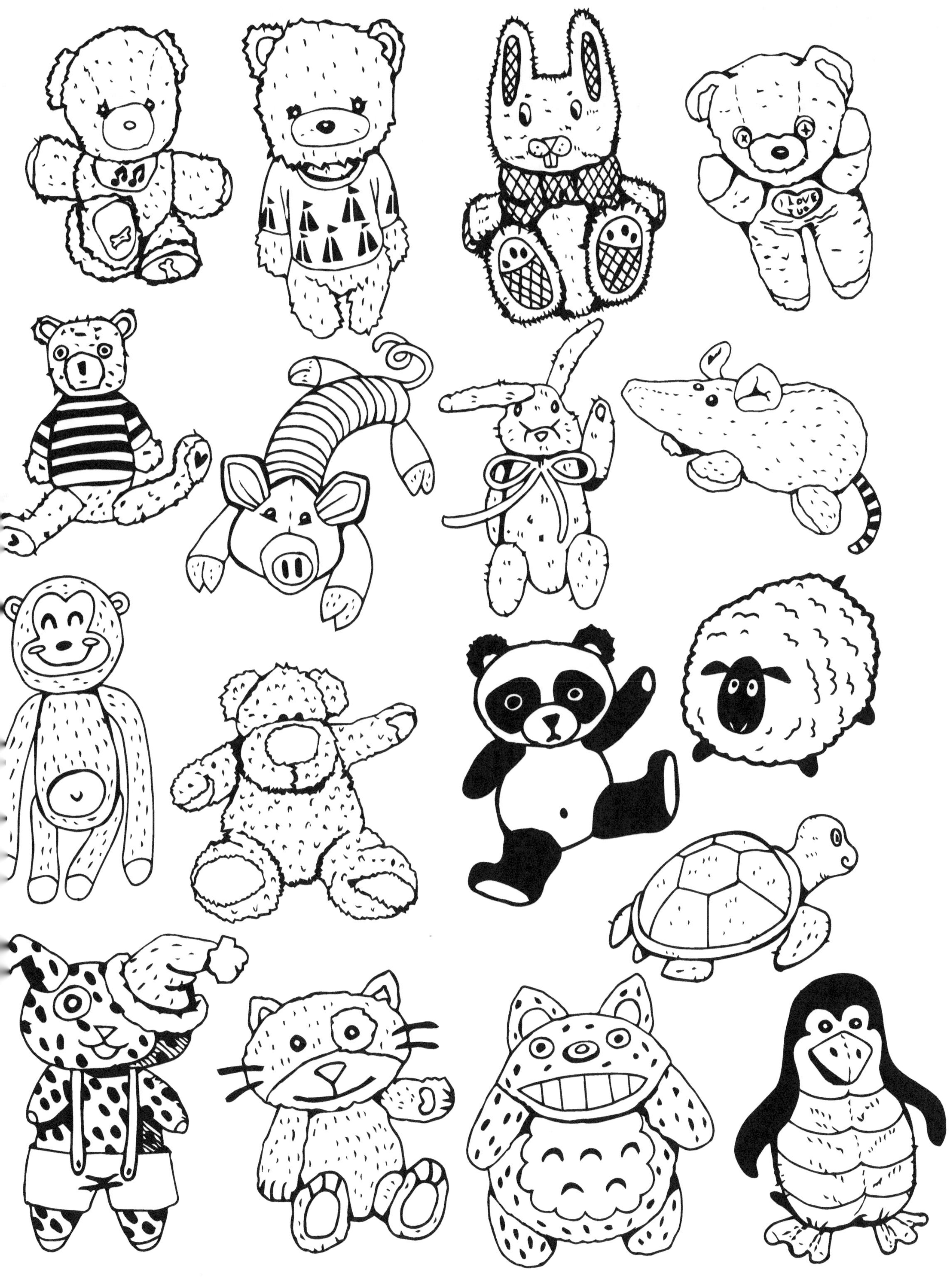

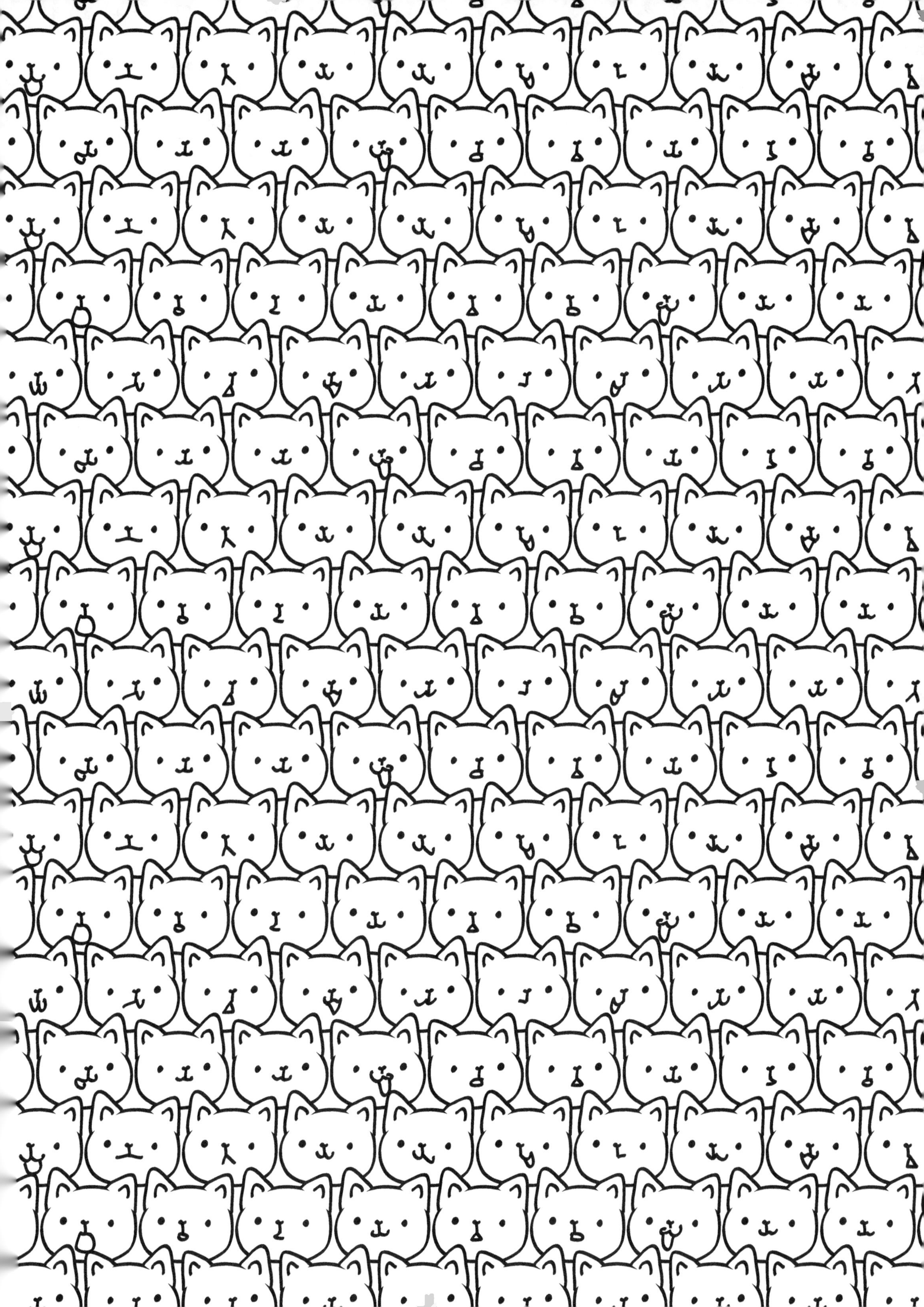

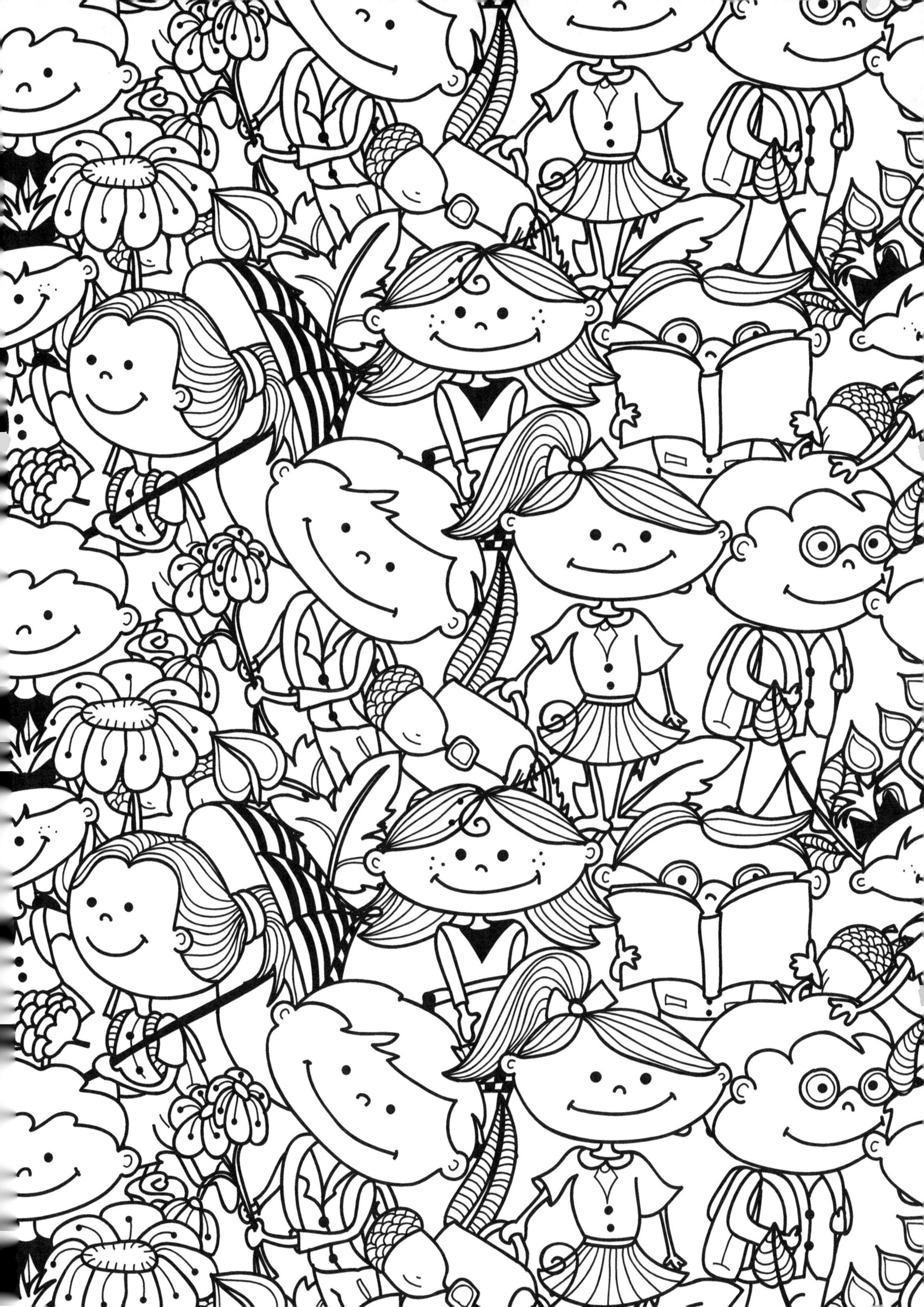

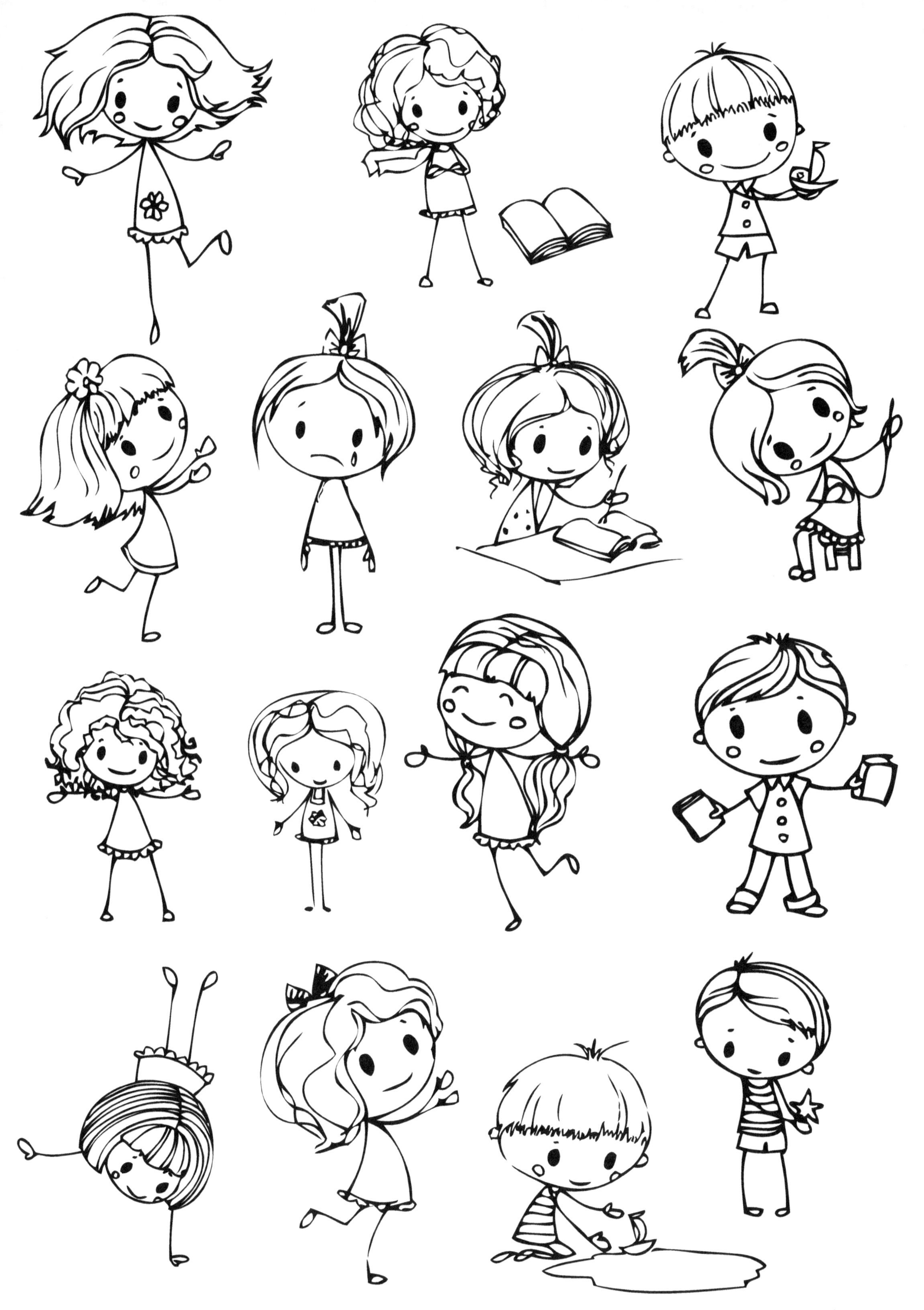

1
2
3
A B
C

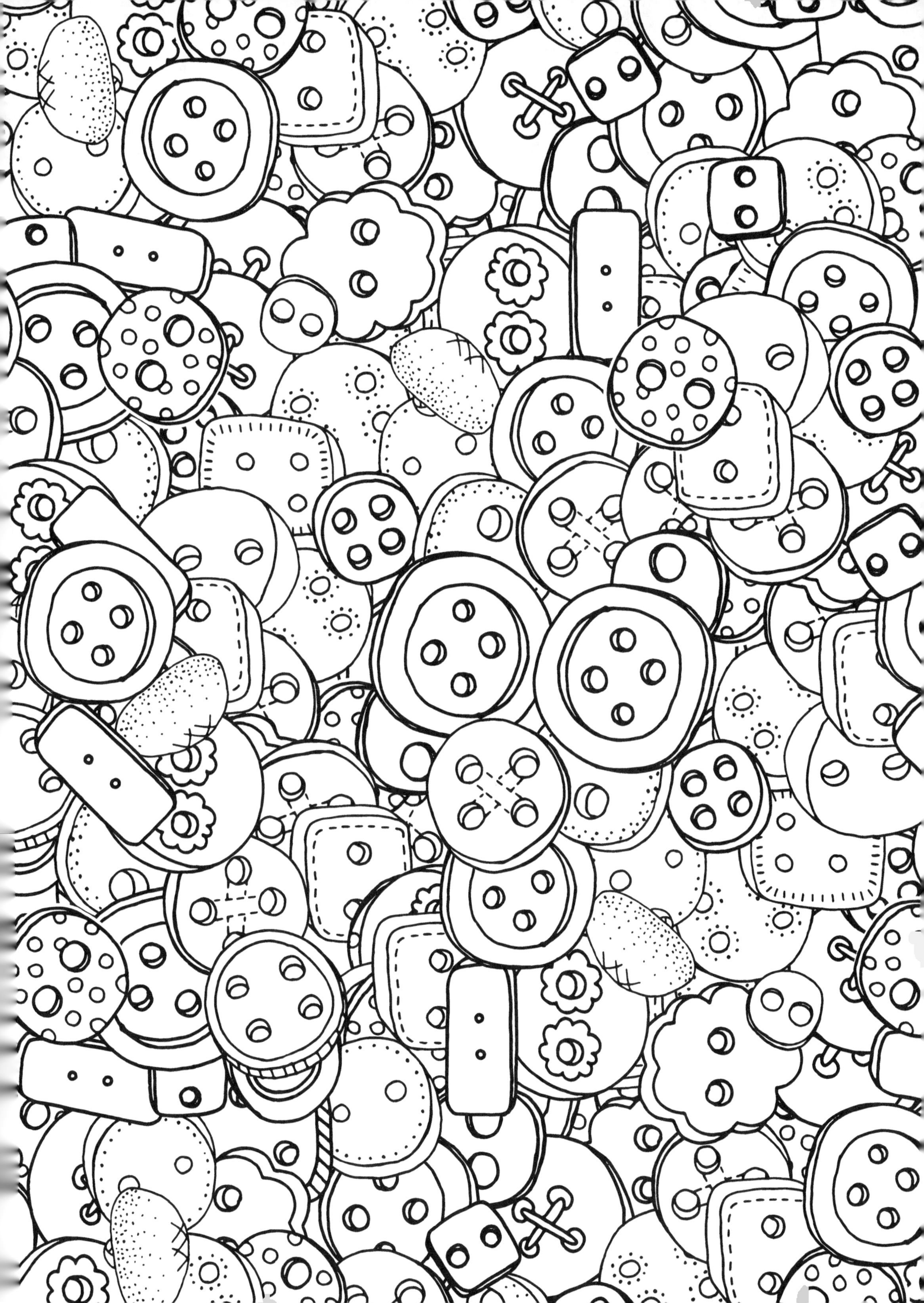

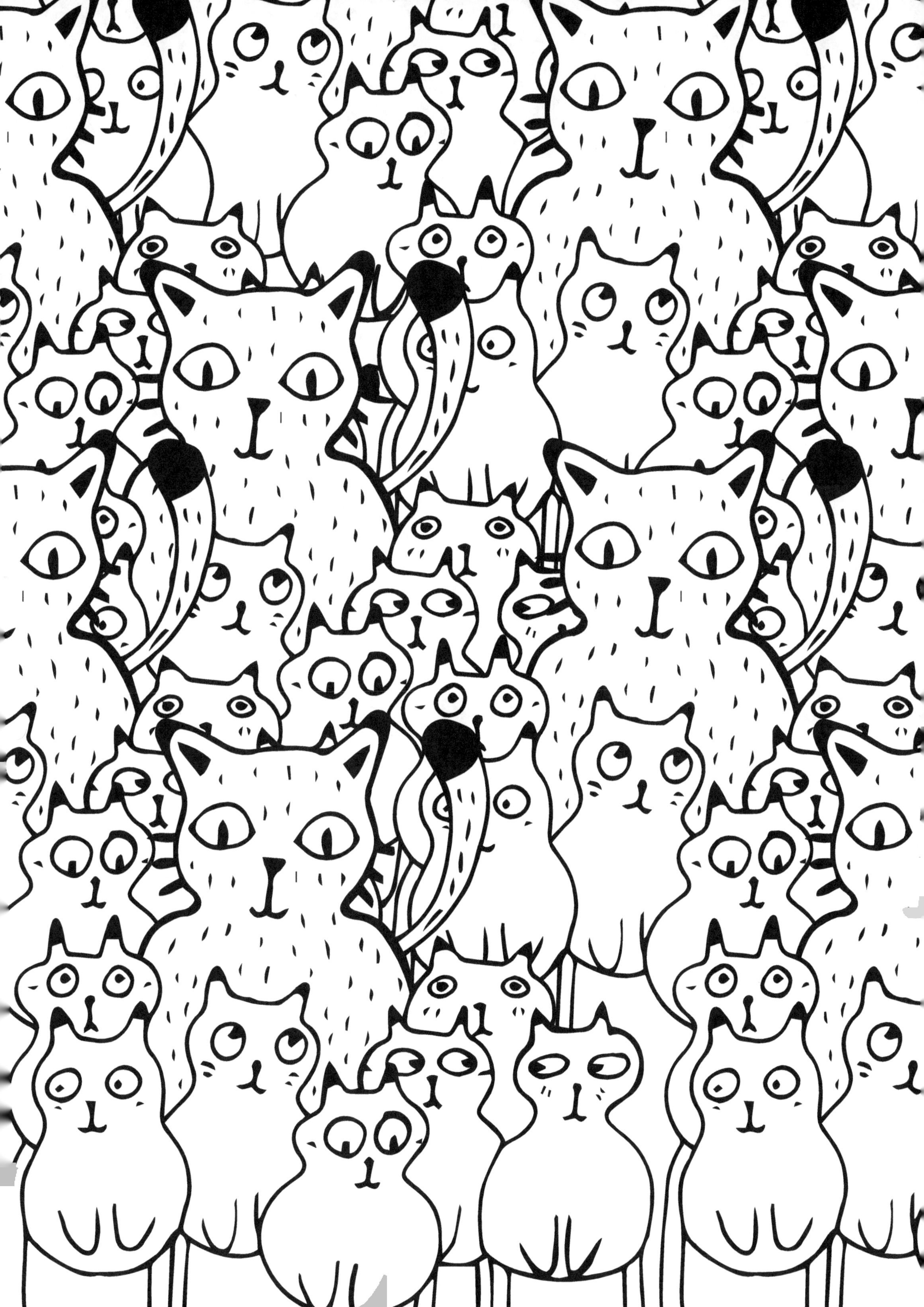

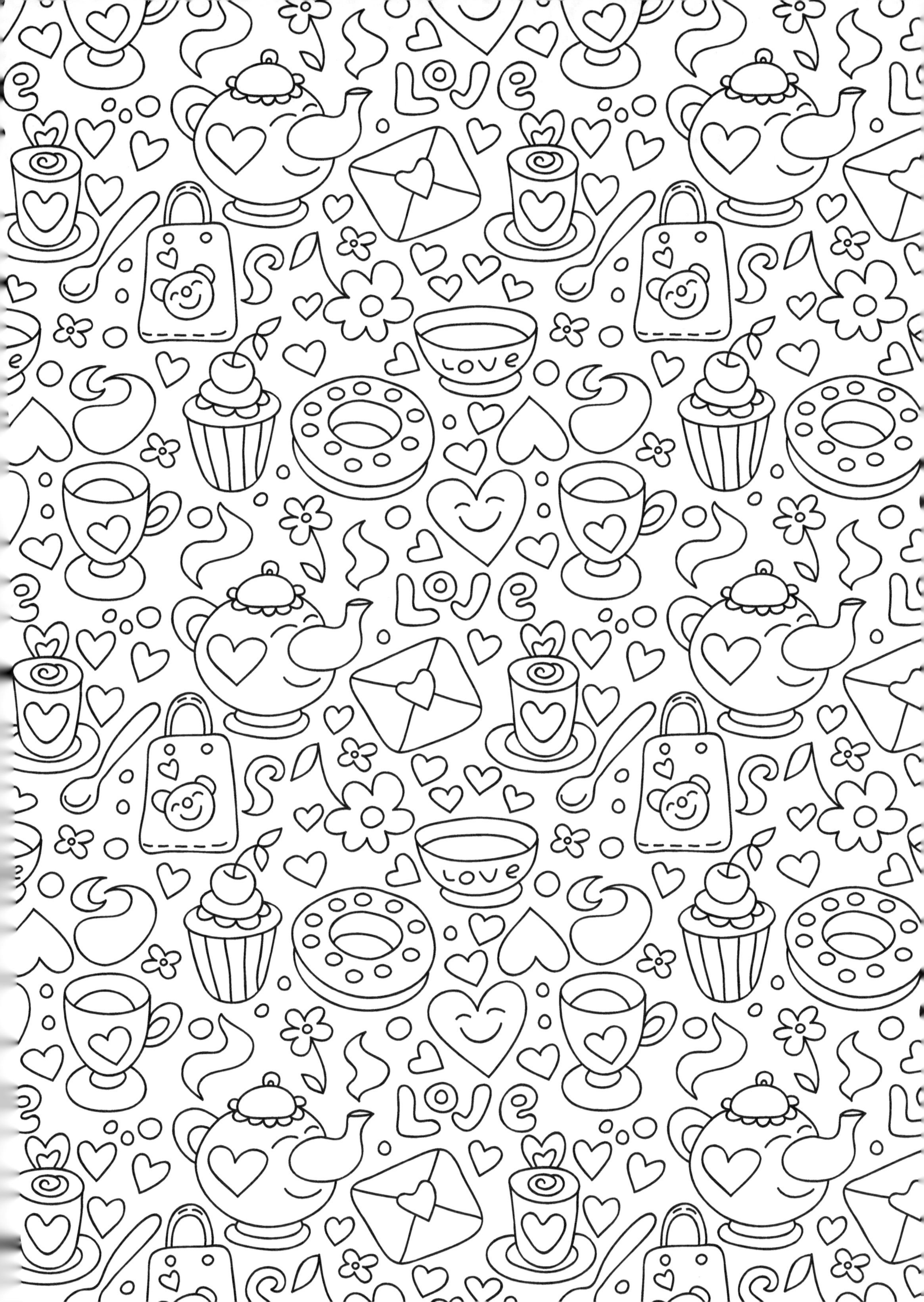
Love
Love
Love
Love
Love

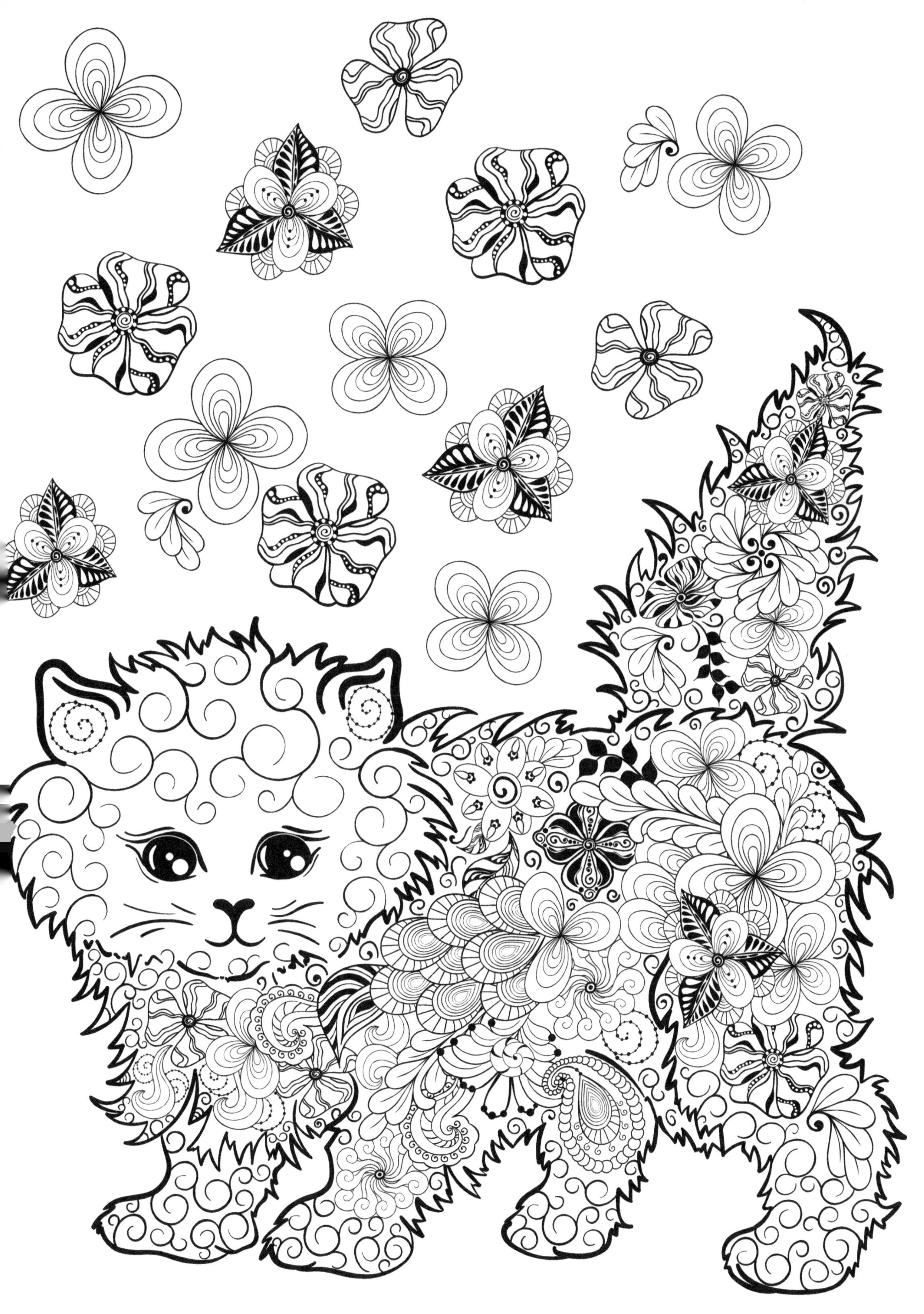

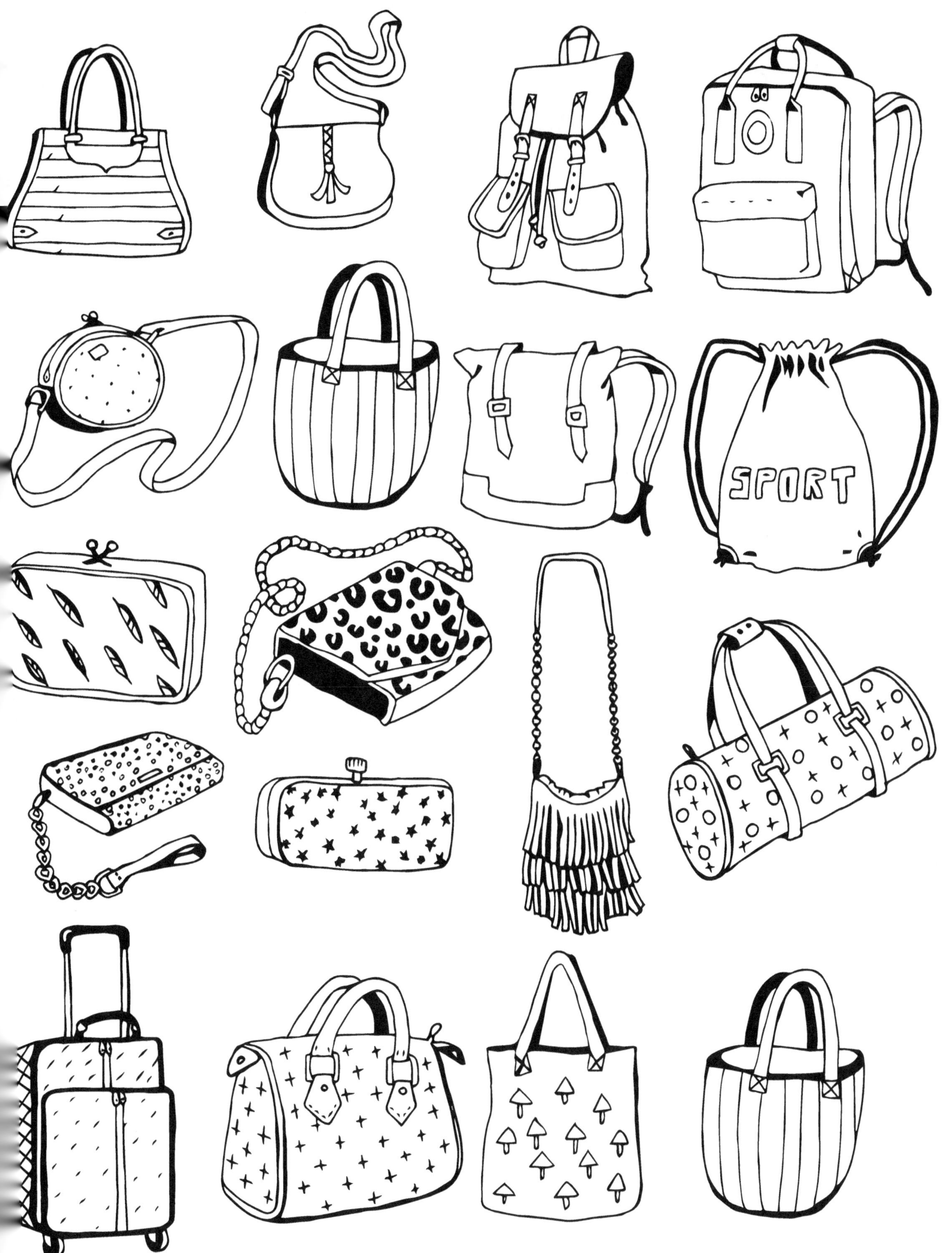
SPORT

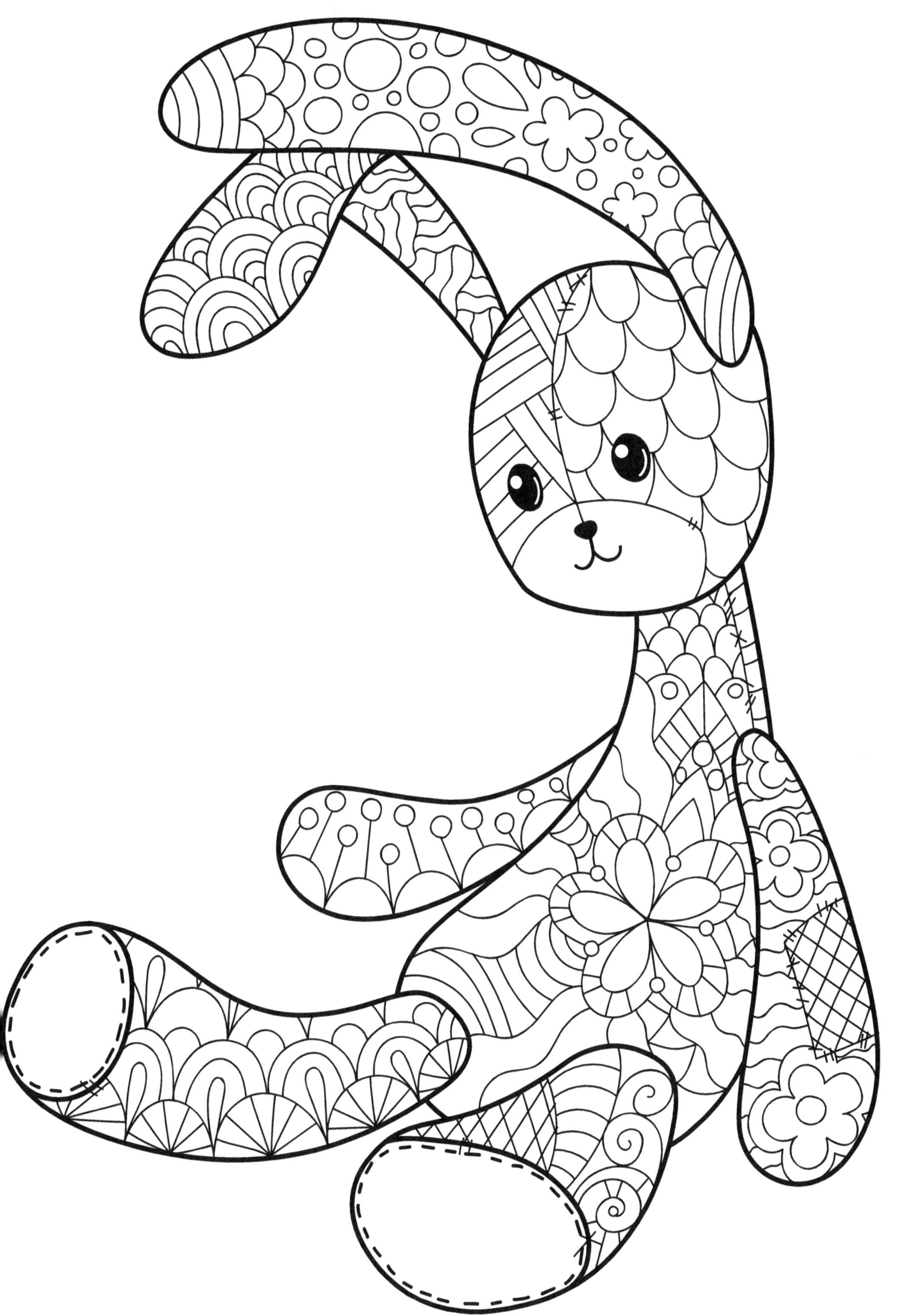

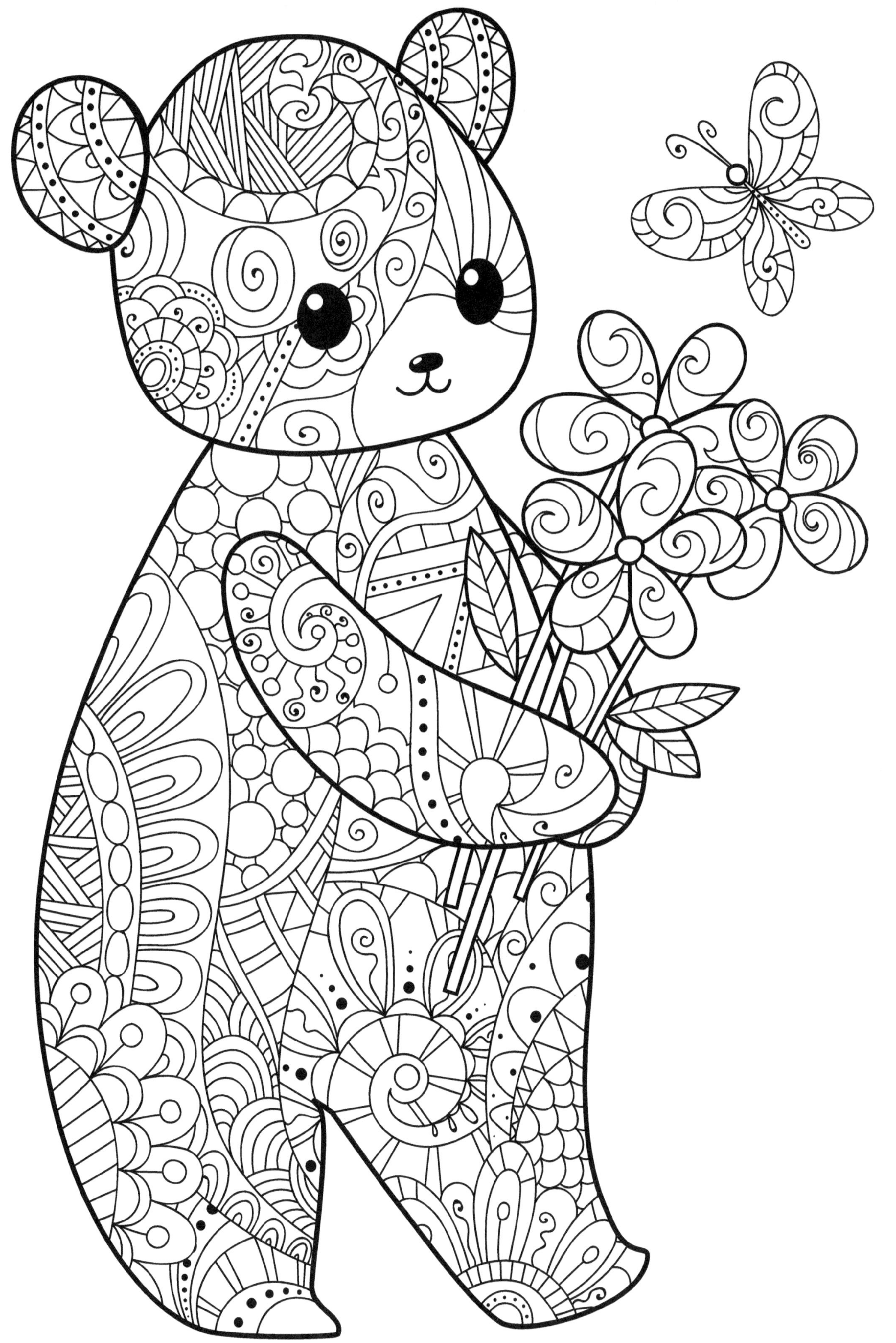

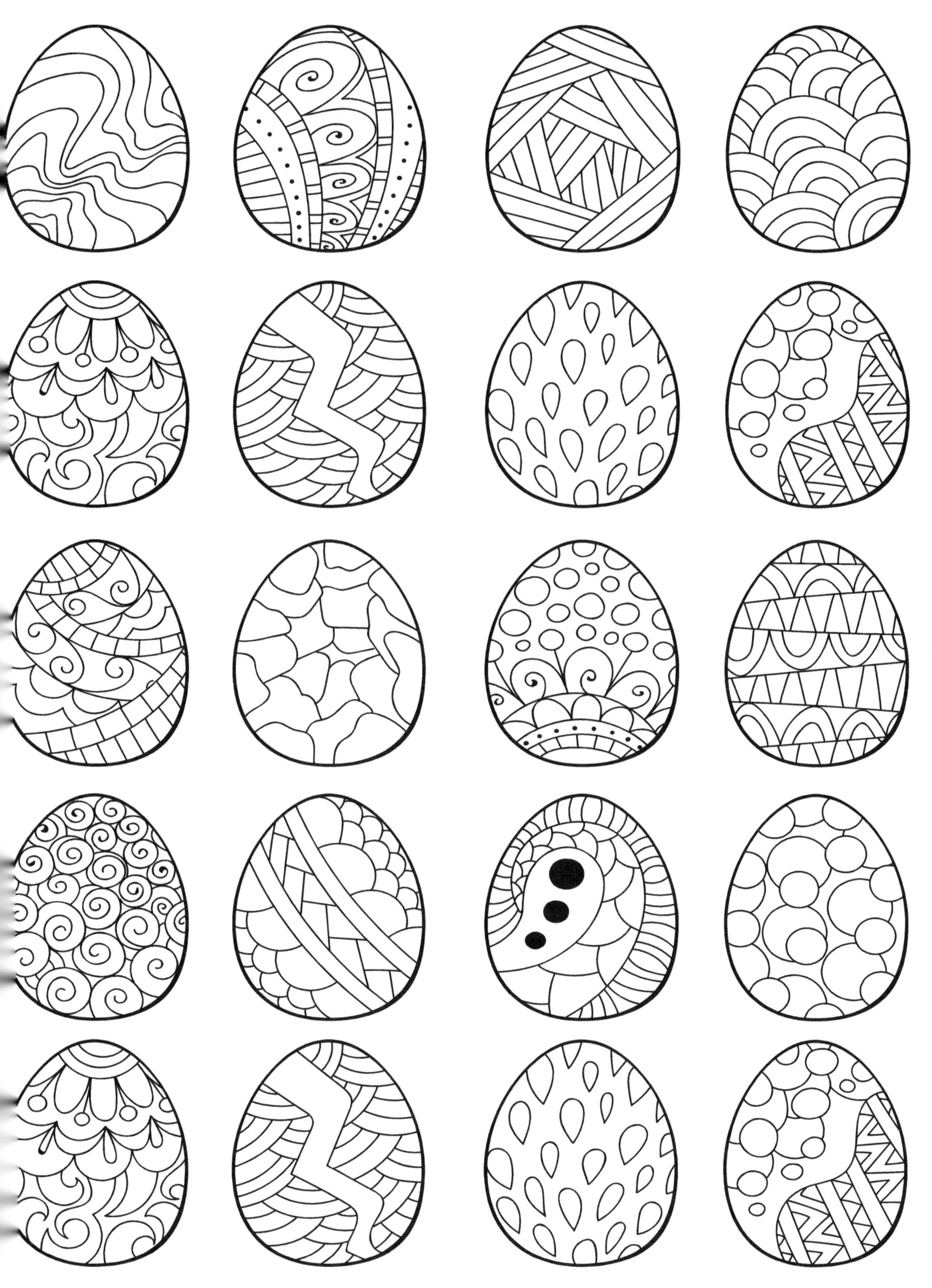

www.ingramcontent.com/pod-product-compliance
Lightning Source LLC
LaVergne TN
LVHW061255100826
845148LV00008B/1136

* 9 7 8 1 7 8 5 9 5 1 2 2 0 *